LEGENDS
OF THE WEST

LEGENDS OF THE WEST

WYATT EARP

John Wukovits

CHELSEA HOUSE PUBLISHERS

Philadelphia

Staff for **WYATT EARP**
Cover Design and Digital Illustration: Alison Burnside
Cover Portrait Credit: Archive Photos
Picture Researcher: Sandy Jones

First Printing

1 3 5 7 9 8 6 4 2

For my daughters—Amy, Julie, and Karen

Library of Congress Cataloging-in-Publication Data

Wukovits, John F., 1944-
    Wyatt Earp / John Wukovits.
        p.   cm. — (Legends of the West)
    Includes bibliographical references and index.
    Summary: Examines the personal life and law enforcement career of the Dodge
City sheriff who always got his man at any cost.
        ISBN 0-7910-3852-1 (hardcover)
        1. Earp, Wyatt, 1848-1929—Juvenile literature. 2. Peace officers—Southwest,
New—Biography—Juvenile literature. 3. United States marshals—Southwest, New--Biogra-
phy—Juvenile literature. 4. Southwest, New—Biography—Juvenile literature. [1. Earp,
Wyatt, 1848-1929. 2. Peace officers.] I. Title. II. Series.
F786.E18W85 1997
978'.02'092—dc21
[B]   97-3941
                                                             CIP
                                                             AC

CONTENTS

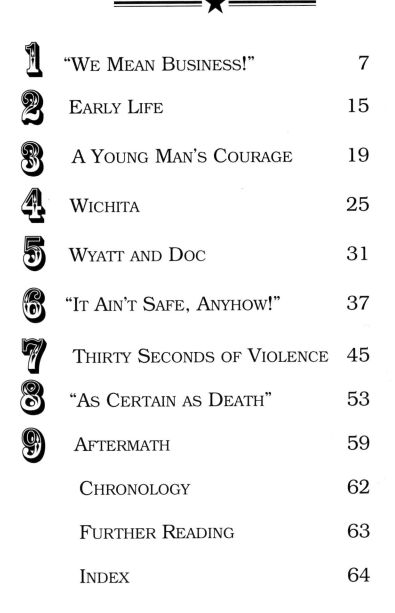

★

1

"WE MEAN BUSINESS!"

In 1876 Dodge City, Kansas was hardly a place for the timid. Standing on the dangerous American frontier, the town attracted rough men accustomed to few comforts and more inclined to shoot first and ask questions later. Gamblers, con artists, and criminals fleeing from the law mingled uneasily with soldiers from nearby Fort Dodge and with women of questionable character. Weary cowboys, exhausted from guiding enormous herds of cattle on the long trek north from Texas, poured into the town's many saloons, eager to spend the money that had recently been paid them in a raucous celebration of drinking, fighting, and gambling.

"Even if you stayed in your room," mentioned one angry railroad executive who stopped in

A picture of Dodge City, Kansas in Wyatt Earp's day. Law and order were frequently absent from such cow towns. The sign to the right warns, "The carrying of Fire Arms strictly prohibited."

Dodge City on his way west, "you couldn't sleep for the noise of yelling and shooting that started about eight o'clock and grew louder until two in the morning. It was terrible."

Order had to be crafted from the chaos, demanded the town's respectable citizens, but how to do that? The lifespan for sheriffs and marshals in the Wild West was dangerously brief, but someone had to assert the law's authority and bring civilization to an uncivilized spot. The town's current crop of lawmen, fearful for their own safety, proved unequal to the task and gave free rein to the cowboys and other revelers.

Mayor George Hoover, pressured to do something, called an emergency meeting of the city council to discuss hiring a new lawman to take charge. The politicians carefully debated the merits of a short list of candidates, but no name attracted enthusiasm until one member mentioned a man who had recently brought law and order to Wichita, another notorious cow town. He had cleaned up the town, some had heard, without relying on a gun. Others related how this law officer had singlehandedly stood up to two feared murderers named Mannie Clements and Ben Thompson and forced them to back down. After a hasty discussion, the city council asked Mayor Hoover to wire this man an offer.

Within one day the Wichita lawman accepted Hoover's invitation. In May of that year, a 6'2", 185-pound man with deep blue eyes, light brown hair, and a large mustache which swooped to the sides slowly rode into town. Elegantly dressed in dark trousers, white shirt, string tie, and a black overcoat that reached to his knees, the man handled himself with the calm assurance that comes from complete self-confidence.

Wyatt Earp, twenty-eight years old and in the infant stages of a career that would bring both glory and criticism, had arrived to tame a lawless place. In the process he would both delight people with his ability to maintain peace and alienate others with his own shady dealings and acquaintances with men and women of unsavory character.

Wyatt first hired three experienced law officers—his younger brother, Morgan Earp, Bat Masterson, and Bat's brother Jim. Good with a gun and calm under pressure, these three provided dependable support for the new marshal. To ensure he could quickly get his hands on adequate firepower when needed, Wyatt placed loaded shotguns in separate buildings about town, including one in the Long Branch Saloon, where he could often be found when not patrolling the streets. Drawn by the excitement and opportunities for profit offered in the West, Earp spent many hours in saloons, where he could gamble and socialize with women.

After inspecting Dodge City, Wyatt saw that the Santa Fe railroad tracks split the town into two distinct halves. Dodge City's business district and its respectable saloons and hotels stood north of the tracks, while to the south lay most of the cheaper establishments which catered to the cowboys. If he could confine the revelers to the south, he would at least give some protection to Dodge City's upright citizens and their businesses, while at the same time he could

Wyatt Earp in his mid-20s. His unique style of law enforcement soon cleaned up Dodge City and other western towns.

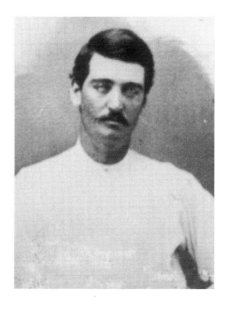

Bat Masterson, close friend and fellow lawman of Wyatt Earp. Their paths frequently crossed in different locations.

start cleaning up the hectic conditions existing in the southern part.

An official notice published in the town newspaper alerted citizens and cowboys alike that a new, tougher system was in place. He declared that from that time on, no guns would be permitted north of the tracks. To avoid arrest, anyone wishing to enter its businesses would first have to check his gun at racks placed in various buildings to avoid arrest. Only law officers could walk the streets armed.

When Earp explained his plan to city officials, he admitted "it will be difficult to enforce this law." One councilman doubted whether he could succeed. Earp mentioned he had accomplished the same in Wichita and that "Dodge City is no different. When the boys learn we mean business, they'll calm down. But I want you gentlemen to know that I am going to be strict about carrying weapons north of the deadline."

Wyatt and his men cautiously patrolled Dodge City's streets over the next few days, wondering how the cowboys would react to the notice. They were sure to be angry, for the new law forced them to hand over something they regarded as much a part of them as their legs or arms. Sooner or later, he knew, someone would step forward to challenge his edict—most likely a drunken cowboy out to gain fame—and Wyatt would have to act quickly and harshly to show who was in charge. So he could be on duty during the most dangerous time—from 6:00 p.m. until daylight—Wyatt slept in the afternoons.

He did not have to wait long. One evening, as Wyatt walked his usual nightly patrol route, four cowboys stumbled out of a saloon north of the tracks. Obviously intoxicated, the noisy men teetered into the street, where one drew his gun and shot out a few street lamps.

"What do you mean, firing a gun here?" questioned Earp. "Don't you know it's against city law?"

"Who, me?" replied the cowboy in a scornful manner. "And what if I do?"

The cowboy quickly had his answer. In an instant, Wyatt advanced and knocked him over the head with his gun, sending him crumbling unconscious to the ground. When a second cowboy stepped toward Earp, Wyatt cracked him, too, across the forehead.

Earp glared at the two remaining cowboys. "Do you boys mean to do any target practice?"

When they backed away, he added, "Well, then, pick up your pals and the whole lot of you get going across the tracks where you belong. Don't come up here again unless you check your guns."

News of the incident electrified the town, impressing both respectable citizens and cowboys alike. That he faced down four armed men and forced them to obey the law was amazing in itself, but that he accomplished this without firing his gun astounded people.

Through his long career, Wyatt rarely resorted to shooting, preferring instead to move close to the lawbreaker, get him talking, then crack him over the head. As he frequently explained to people, "I would rather knock them unconscious than kill them. Any man, out making a fool of himself, would rather wake up the next day with a pounding headache than be dead." However, Earp was not averse to shooting if the situation called for it.

The cowboys now knew they could not lightly dismiss Earp as they had done with previous lawmen. Still, the challenges continued. One time Wyatt heard that a group of cowboys was riding toward Dodge City from their cattle camp, planning on shooting up the town. He grabbed one of his shotguns and strode toward the bridge which arched across the Arkansas River, stood in the center of the street, and waited for the group to arrive.

Before long, forty riders appeared on the bridge's far end and started across. Word of the encounter had spread through town, and a large crowd of onlookers had gathered to see what would happen to their brash law officer. Earp stood like a rock and cradled the shotgun in his left arm as the cowboys drew closer. The riders finally halted within yards of Earp, who bellowed, "You boys better turn around and go home. Leave your guns there, then come along back and have your fun."

A moment of strained silence followed. Two deputies, who had arrived just after Wyatt, stood yards behind their leader with their weapons ready. Sensing that Earp would not back down, the riders slowly turned around and headed back to camp.

After this incident the remainder of the cattle season, about eight months, passed without serious difficulty. Cowboys either remained south of the tracks or checked their guns before crossing to the north. Amazingly, only two men were killed in drunken fights compared to seventy in the previous four years, and neither Wyatt nor any man on his force resorted to shooting anyone. Mayor Hoover and the rest of town breathed easier now that law and order, in the person of Marshal Earp, had transformed

Dodge City into a pleasant place in which to live.

Even Ned Buntline, noted author of dime novels, which were hastily written books extolling the exploits of western lawmen and criminals, arrived to present a special gun to Wyatt. Called the Buntline Special, the .45-caliber gun sported a twelve-inch barrel, perfect for Wyatt's preference for knocking out drunken cowboys. Earp carried this gun with him for the next twenty-five years.

Restless now that Dodge City had been tamed, Wyatt looked elsewhere for excitement and opportunities for profit. He found it in the Black Hills in the Dakota Territory, where gold had recently been found. Resigning his post as marshal, Wyatt headed north to continue a personal saga that began twenty-eight years earlier in Illinois.

Main Street in Dodge City. Earp walked this and the other streets each night to keep the peace.

EARLY LIFE

Wyatt Earp was born on March 19, 1848 in Monmouth, Illinois, the fifth of eight children born to Nicholas and Virginia Earp. Nicholas, who had served in the Mexican War shortly before Wyatt's birth, named his son after the sergeant with whom he had fought and whom he had grown to admire. As a result of this military background, Nicholas emphasized two qualities to his sons—the ability to defend oneself and loyalty to family and friends.

When Wyatt was two years old, Nicholas moved the family to Pella, Iowa and started a pattern of constant motion which followed Wyatt throughout his life. Wyatt rarely remained long enough in one spot to develop deep ties to any community. Instead, he would settle in for a time, then head out for new challenges and opportunities. As a result, loyalty to family and the small number of close friendships he formed became increasingly important.

The home in Monmouth, Illinois where Wyatt Earp lived. Two years after his birth, the family moved to Iowa.

Pella also gave young Wyatt his first taste of frontier living where, in the absence of established law and order, matters were frequently settled by the individuals involved, mainly through use of a six-shooter. Nicholas reminded his boys that since the law could often not protect them, they would have to help each other in times of crisis and would have to become expert at using weapons.

When the Civil War split the nation in two in 1861, Nicholas and his three oldest sons—Newton, James, and Virgil—joined the Union Army to fight against the South. Though eager to serve alongside his family, the thirteen-year-old Wyatt stayed behind to run the 80-acre farm with brothers Morgan and Warren. Once Wyatt ran off to enlist, but Nicholas learned about it and had him sent back home.

After completing his service three years later, Nicholas sold the farm, packed the family belongings into two covered wagons, and headed for California. Though the difficult seven-month trip challenged everyone's ability to endure hardships, Wyatt received his first glimpse of the opportunities available in the wide open West, where it seemed that any person willing to risk his life and possessions could turn a handy profit.

Nicholas took the family to the San Bernardino area in the middle of California, where he started a ranch. Wyatt picked up odd jobs in addition to working on the family ranch, including driving a stagecoach east across the Mojave Desert to Arizona and west from San Bernardino to Los Angeles.

Though Wyatt loved roaming the open lands of the West, an individual back in Monmouth drew him home. In 1870, he returned to Illinois to court the lovely Willa Sutherland, whom he married later in the year. The happy couple made plans to start a farm and raise a family, but tragedy blocked those dreams when, only three and one half months after the wedding, Willa became ill during a typhus epidemic and died. The heartbroken Wyatt, with no ties holding him to Illinois, again headed west to seek opportunity and peace.

He found little but trouble for two years. For a time he hunted buffalo to provide food for mapping expeditions into Indian Territory, which is now the state of Oklahoma. During this period he met a man who became one of his closest friends—William Barclay "Bat" Masterson—but no one seemed able to lift him out of the depression into which he sank over losing his wife.

He plunged to the lowest part of his life on March 28, 1871 when authorities in Indian Territory arrested Wyatt for horse theft, a crime that often brought death to the guilty. Wyatt avoided the consequence when, after being set free on bond, he immediately fled the area. Though outside the reach of lawmen from Indian Territory, Wyatt did little more than drift in and out of various frontier towns in Kansas, where he spent most of his time drinking and gambling in saloons.

Finally, in early 1873, he turned to the profession which would bring him both fame and notoriety—enforcing the law.

A YOUNG MAN'S COURAGE

Wyatt landed his first job as peace offi-cer almost by accident. In 1873 he rode into Ellsworth, Kansas, a small town that swelled each summer with Texas cat-tle and the cowboys that brought them along the long, dusty trail to Kansas railroad stops for transport east. After months of hard work, the cowboys poured into Ellsworth looking for whiskey, women, and wild times.

Ellsworth accommodated them. Saloons, dance halls, and gambling rooms dominated the town. Law-abiding citizens learned to stay out of the cowboys' way, who thought nothing of getting drunk, staggering out into the dusty street, and shooting at anything that drifted into

Like many men who headed west, Ben Thompson straddled both sides of the law. He and Wyatt tan-gled in Ellsworth.

their blurry-eyed view.

As many as 1,500 cowboys might swarm on Ellsworth in any given summer week. One popular story of the time claimed that though all cowboys were not from Texas, they were called Texans because, "they all live up to the saying that 'every hoss from Texas will buck, and every

Ellsworth, Kansas, a small cow town that saw plenty of excitement when the cowboys roared in each summer.

man from Texas will fight.'"

How Wyatt first became involved in law enforcement is not clear. As is true with many figures who dominate the pages of Western history, facts intertwine with myth to produce a legend that, while difficult to know where truth stops and myth begins, establishes a reputation.

According to the story, two gunfighters who loved to take drunken cowboys' money in rigged gambling schemes, Ben and Bill Thompson, arrived in Ellsworth. Because of the Thompson brothers' skill with weapons and their mean tempers, few had the courage–or stupidity–to challenge them. Bat Masterson told Wyatt to be on guard whenever the brothers appeared, because "wherever they set themselves up, they think they own the town. According to them, their word is law."

One day, a drunken Ben and Bill Thompson stormed into the street searching for an acquaintance who supposedly owed them money. Ellsworth's sheriff, Chauncey B. Whitney, cautiously edged out from the sidewalk to talk some sense into the brothers, but as he stepped nearer, Bill Thompson fired both barrels of his shotgun directly at the lawman. As Whitney collapsed in a bloody heap, Ben shouted that he would cover Bill while he fled Ellsworth.

Ben then walked into a saloon with several fellow Texans and ordered another drink. Mayor James Miller pled with Ben to peacefully surrender his weapon, but Thompson refused. Here is where the incident dissolves into a mixture of fact and myth. Most witnesses agree that Thompson eventually handed over his weapon to Miller after the mayor fired several law officers who planned to shoot it out with the cowboy.

However, some versions claim that Wyatt apprehended Thompson. Angered that he could not get a haircut without gunshots ringing about the street, Wyatt stomped out of the barber shop and wondered what the fuss was all about.

"It's none of my business," replied Earp when he learned the cause of the commotion, "but if it was me I'd get me a gun and arrest Ben Thompson or kill him."

Miller handed Wyatt a badge and dared him to arrest Thompson. Unfazed by the challenge, Wyatt stepped into the street.

"What are you doing, kid?" wondered the bleary-eyed Thompson.

"Throw down your guns and tell your pals to keep out of this," answered Wyatt, as he inched within fifteen yards of the gunman.

When Ben muttered that he would "rather talk than fight," Wyatt claimed, "I'll get you either way, Ben. I'll either kill you or take you to jail."

Thompson indicated he might be willing to put down his gun, but he feared that one of the lawmen watching might then take aim at him.

"Not while you're my prisoner," stated Wyatt. "Anybody that gets you will have to get me, too."

With these words of assurance, Thompson tossed his shotgun into the street, burst out in laughter, and surrendered to Earp. When Bat Masterson asked Thompson later why he had dropped his weapon, Ben replied that Earp "woulda killed me if I hadn't. And then my buddies woulda got him." Adding that he admired the young man's courage, Ben stated he decid-

Situated on the wide-open Kansas plains, Ellsworth offered few comforts to its settlers.

ed to end the matter with no further gunplay.

Some historians claim Earp was not even in town at the time of this incident, but it is an example of how fact and myth have become so tangled that it is sometimes difficult to pinpoint exactly which feats Wyatt Earp accomplished and which are pure fantasy. In any case, Wyatt's reputation as a fearless lawman, who would rather talk a man into putting down his gun rather than resort to shooting it out, began in Ellsworth.

His close friend, Bat Masterson, marveled at Earp's apparent lack of fear in deadly situations. "Wyatt Earp is one of the few men I personally knew in the West in the early days, whom I regarded as absolutely destitute of physical fear....no one has ever humiliated this man Earp." He added that "there were few men in the West who could whip Earp in a rough-and-tumble fight."

Some cowboys scoffed that they could handle the young lawman. They learned differently, though, not only in Ellsworth but in Wichita, Kansas.

WICHITA

In April, 1875 Wyatt accepted the post of deputy marshal in Wichita, Kansas, another in the string of wild cowtowns that plagued certain portions of the American West. The city offered $125 a month, a substantial amount for those days, and in return Wyatt agreed to maintain the peace, collect fines from lawbreakers, and hand over the money to city leaders.

As in Ellsworth, Earp's record in Wichita is spotted with controversy. While some accounts ascribe heroic deeds to the marshal, others accuse Earp of crass dishonesty and failure to perform his duty. The truth most likely rests somewhere in the middle.

According to Earp's supporters, he cleaned up Wichita in the same manner he straightened out Ellsworth. Earp's first step was to assert the law's authority by standing up to a cowboy in a classic confrontation.

Wichita, Kansas in the 1870s. As its deputy marshal, Earp had to stand up to an array of reckless cowboys to maintain law and order.

One day a wealthy Texas cattle rancher named Abel "Shanghai" Pierce stumbled into the street and began shouting profanities. Few who knew the man were willing to oppose him, as Pierce was not only a powerful cattleman but, at six feet four inches tall and 220 pounds, he posed quite an obstacle. Wyatt, however, managed to take away his gun, and he warned Pierce to settle down or he would have to arrest him.

Things quieted for a while, but a few hours later Pierce was back outside, shooting up the streets with a group of cowboy friends. Earp carefully circled behind the men, pointed a shotgun at Pierce, and ordered everyone to drop their weapons. Realizing that he would be the first man shot if they did not follow Earp's instructions, Pierce told his men to obey. Wyatt led the group to court, where a judge dished out stiff fines to each man.

To get revenge, Pierce and his men supposedly hired a notorious murderer named Mannie Clements to kill the deputy marshal. When Earp learned that Clements and about forty cowboys were riding toward town, he lined up a posse along Wichita's main street. Before long Clements appeared, a gun in each hand, walking at the head of his group. Wyatt stepped toward Clements, leveled an icy gaze toward him, and in a steady voice told him to head back to camp. Like Pierce before him, Clements realized that once trouble began, he would be the first man gunned down by Earp, so after some strained moments of inaction, Clements and the cowboys backed away and returned to camp. This, according to Earp supporters, was the last time the cowboys disrupted Wichita's peace.

Other records paint a different picture. Some

historians claim Earp never faced down Clements. They assert that he merely made routine arrests in his year on the job, and in fact landed in trouble with the city commission by failing to hand over a hefty amount in fines that he had collected from lawbreakers. The longest story appearing in the Wichita newspaper during Earp's tenure detailed the marshal's

Another view of Wichita while Earp worked there.

arrest, fining, and firing by the city commission for disturbing the peace on April 5, 1876, when he punched an election opponent who was running against Earp for the post of city marshal. Official Wichita records show that on April 19, 1876 the city commission voted against rehiring Wyatt Earp for another year, and the next month recommended that the vagrancy law be enforced against him. However, by that time Wyatt had already started for his next destination—Dodge City, Kansas.

Though the controversial lawman displayed a tendency to ruffle the feathers of both those for whom he supposedly worked as well as those he was hired to supervise, Wyatt Earp proved to be no different than most men attracted by the West, where the opportunity for quick profit existed side by side with danger. This combination normally draws men and women who are either outright criminals or who possess a combination of decency with a willingness to act outside the law to protect their own interests. Men who might normally be law-abiding citizens in Ohio or New York would have thought little of taking the law into their own hands in Kansas, Arizona, or the Dakotas.

Depending upon the situation, Earp either enforced the law on lawbreakers, used the law in his own behalf, or acted outside the law. This dual strain—savagery mildly tamed by civilization—appeared in many characters who populated the West.

A sign posted above a ramshackle saloon that served whiskey to rough-edged miners illustrated this odd combination. In large letters, the sign urged, "DON'T FORGET TO WRITE TO MOTHER. SHE IS THINKING OF YOU. WE FURNISH PAPER AND ENVELOPES FREE, AND

HAVE THE BEST WHISKEY IN TOWN."

Earp existed in a violent world where the law was only beginning to make inroads. He proved to be no worse, and no better, than most of his contemporaries.

WYATT AND DOC

By the time Wyatt arrived in Deadwood, South Dakota, following his first stint as Dodge City law officer, all the promising claims had already been taken. Rather than give up, he saw an opportunity. Winter was fast approaching, meaning that prospectors would need wood for fires. He purchased large amounts at a distant location, then hauled it to the Deadwood region in a wagon and resold the wood at a large profit. By spring of 1877, Earp had earned $5,000, showing what would be a lifelong ability to make money through sharp business practices.

With spring's arrival, Earp hired on with Wells Fargo as a stagecoach guard. At Cheyenne, one of the coach's stops, Wyatt found a telegram from Dodge City's mayor, pleading for his hasty return. The riotous cowboys, having completed

John Henry "Doc" Holliday, Wyatt's close friend. Though a ruthless killer with a violent temper, he and Wyatt helped each other on many occasions.

another long cattle drive from Texas, again hounded the town with their loud celebrations and constant fistfights. Citizens soon tired of what they called the cowboys' practice of "killing a man for breakfast every morning." Wyatt agreed to resume his post and was soon on his way back to Dodge City.

The marshal arrived in July and began enforcing the no-gun law with brutal efficiency. Each person who broke that law received a $2.50 fine, and by month's end over $1,000 in fines had been collected. As was the custom at the time, Earp and his deputies received a portion of each fine, so July proved to be a profitable month for Earp. Townspeople relaxed that with their marshal back on the job, peace would shortly reappear.

He still had much work to do, even with the town's females. The Dodge City *Times* described one incident. "Miss Frankie Bell who wears the belt for superiority in point of muscular ability, heaped epithets upon the unoffending head of Mr. Wyatt Earp to such an extent as to provoke a slap from" Earp. Miss Bell spent the night in jail for her outburst.

Though pleased with Earp's calming presence, some citizens disapproved of Wyatt's recent friendship with twenty-nine-year-old John Henry "Doc" Holliday, a notorious gambler and gunman. A former dentist from Atlanta, Doc Holliday traveled west to seek relief from the ravages of tuberculosis in the region's healthier atmosphere. Because of the disease's destructiveness, Holliday looked far older than his years. Dark, sunken sockets held lifeless eyes that stared out from a whitened face.

Holliday's horrendous temper landed him in difficult spots. He had been in numerous gunfights, including scrapes in which he had killed a soldier and two civilians in Texas. As a result, police from five different locations issued warrants for his arrest. After checking into the Dodge House in Dodge City, Holliday's tantrums caused so many problems that the manager and other workers were afraid to deal with him.

In spite of this, Wyatt formed a close bond with Holliday, most likely because the lawman shared some characteristics with the lawbreaker. Like Earp, Holliday's courage could never be doubted, and Wyatt knew he could always count on his friend in a tight spot. Bat Masterson later explained that Doc's "whole heart and soul were wrapped up in Wyatt Earp and he was always ready to stake his life in defense of any cause in which Wyatt was interested."

The seedier characters inhabiting Dodge City south of the tracks hated Earp's return. Rumors bounced around that a wealthy cattleman had offered a large sum of money to anyone who could kill the marshal. Though Earp scoffed at the notion, a dangerous murderer by the name of Clay Allison tried to goad Wyatt into a gunfight shortly after the lawman returned. Earp succeeded in disarming Allison and running him out of town.

Another rancher, Tobe Driskill, stood up to Earp in 1878 with similar results. One evening Driskill rode into town with a large group of cowboys and barged into the Long Branch Saloon, ready to start a wild night. When he spotted Wyatt standing at the far end of the bar, Driskill drew his gun and loudly threatened the marshal. Earp, caught off guard, could do nothing but let the drama unfold.

Tense seconds ticked by as Earp quietly let Driskill have his say. Suddenly, Doc Holliday

Wyatt Earp as a marshal in Dodge City.

crashed through the door with revolvers in both hands. When Driskill turned toward the commotion, Earp yanked out his gun and cracked Driskill across the skull, then dragged the unconscious cattleman to jail.

Earp survived a third attempt on his life shortly afterward. While Earp stood outside the Comique Theater one evening, a rider named George Hoyt, supposedly after the reward money, charged down the street and fired three shots at the marshal. Though missing their target, the bullets tore through the theater's walls and sent patrons scattering for cover, including famed entertainer Eddie Foy. When Foy returned to his dressing room, he found that a brand new suit that had been hanging in the room "had been penetrated by three bullets, and one of them had started a ring of fire smoldering around the hole."

By 1879 Dodge City had once again become too civilized for Wyatt Earp. Eager for action and wary of opponents' bullets, he resigned in the fall of 1879, declaring, "I'm tired of being a target." He looked toward a small town in the Arizona Territory to the southwest that supposedly offered both wealth from nearby silver deposits and excitement from its raw frontier spirit. Earp set out to seek fortune in Tombstone, Arizona. Instead, he found fame.

"IT AIN'T SAFE, ANYHOW!"

Wyatt did not travel to Tombstone alone. His brother James, and James's family, accompanied him. They met brother Virgil, who had recently been appointed deputy U.S. marshal for the Tombstone area, when they reached Prescott, Arizona. They then continued toward their destination, where a month after their arrival they were joined by brother Morgan and Doc Holliday. Though Virgil was the marshal, as always Wyatt dominated family actions through his bearing and reputation.

Not even one year old by the time Wyatt and his brothers arrived, Tombstone relied upon rich silver mines in the hills beyond for its wealth. With large amounts of money and power at stake, violence and death were sure to follow.

Morgan Earp

The Tombstone *Epitaph* reported their arrival in glowing terms. "Tall, gaunt, and intrepid, they [the Earps] caused considerable comment when they first arrived, particularly because of Wyatt's reputation as a peace officer in Dodge City, Kansas. All the cattle rustlers in Kansas, Colorado, New Mexico, and western Texas knew and feared Wyatt Earp."

Tombstone presented little to look at when the Earps first rode into town in early December, 1879, but then that should hardly be surprising for a town with such a despairing name. According to the most accepted story, Tombstone received its name from an early prospector who decided to brave the hazards of the dangerous lands near the Mexican border in hopes of striking it rich in nearby silver-laden hills. Wealth awaited those hardy souls who could tap into the enormous lode of metal, but so did the feared Apaches, who roamed the area at will. An Army officer stared at the prospector as if he were insane and warned, "The only stone you'll find in those parts will be your own tombstone."

Barely ten months old in Decembe, the town consisted mainly of tents and hastily erected wooden shacks, populated by rough-looking prospectors purchasing equipment from store-owners who had only recently opened businessess. Gamblers and con artists slipped in and out of establishments, trying to swindle gullible men out of their money, while saloonkeepers tempted each newcomer with free-flowing whiskey and loose women.

Violence frequently shattered an uneasy peace. One of the town's newspapers, the Tombstone *Nugget*, complained that wild prospectos and their "lewd women" too often spilled out into the streets and shot up the town. "We live mostly in canvas houses up here, and when lunatics like those who fired so promiscuously the other night are on the rampage, it ain't safe, anyhow!"

A local attorney and Earp friend, Wells Spicer, wrote that Tombstone contained two dance halls, twelve gambling establishments, and over twenty saloons, but he had faith that civilization would eventually tame the area. "There is hope, for I know of two Bibles in Town."

Over one hundred new settlers moved into Tombstone each day in 1880, causing John P. Clum, editor of the *Epitaph*, to predict the city's population would swell to 10,000 by the year's end. The *Epitaph* and its competitor, the *Nugget*, vied for readers in the rapidly expanding community, which was named county seat when Cochise County was organized.

Virgil Earp

Four main streets—Safford, Fremont, Allen, and Toughnut—ran parallel to one another, while 2nd, 3rd, 4th, 5th, and 6th Streets crossed at right angles. Important establishments dotted the layout, including a courthouse, city hall, and Episcopal church, the Crystal Palace Saloon and its main rival, The Oriental Salon, and the modern day equivalent to a parking lot, where a cowboy could rest and berth his horse—the O.K. Corral.

Played out against such a backdrop were the events leading to the confrontation erroneously known to history as the "Gunfight at the O.K. Corral." The drama started when a crazed cowboy murdered Tombstone's marshal. Virgil succeeded the slain lawman, which gave the Earp brothers a power base in town.

In addition, Wyatt craftily built a minor eco-

James Earp

nomic empire. Shortly after settling in Tombstone, he bought into a silver mine and purchased a share of the town's most profitable
gambling house, The Oriental Saloon. In addition, he ran nightly card games across the street
at the Eagle Brewery, where he pocketed a tidy
sum. Since Wyatt served as Virgil's assistant
marshal, he could run out of town anyone disturbing either saloon or any gambler who might
object to how the games were conducted. Wyatt
and his brothers intended to protect such a profitable arrangement by almost any means, including guns.

Wyatt supposedly earned so much money
that by March of 1880, he sold his portion of
the silver mine for $30,000. As such, he natu-
rally associated with Tombstone's businessmen
and bankers, men who invested money and gen-
erally voted for the Republican Party.

This placed Earp in opposition to the area's
other major faction—Cochise County's ranchers, labeled cowboys by John Clum's *Epitaph*,
which supported Earp. These men had settled
in the Tombstone region years before the businessmen and resented the sudden arrival of so
many newcomers like Earp. They worked the
land rather than simply invested in it; cattle—
their lifeblood—needed wide open spaces, yet
in their midst a thriving city gobbled up pre-
cious land.

Bitterness between the two groups flared
each time another throng of entertainment-
starved cowboys rode in to threaten Tombstone's
peace. The town's citizens hated the constant
celebrating, frequent gunplay, and wild disregard for others' rights. They chafed at the ranchers' attitude that the Tombstone area belonged
to them, not these pesky newcomers. Wyatt

Earp, particularly, had no use for cowboys, since he had experienced little but trouble from them wherever he had lived. Armed with guns and badges, Wyatt Earp and his brothers in effect became enforcers for the town's establishment.

They would not get their way without a fight, though, as the ranchers were just as determined to protect their interests. Led by Joseph Isaac "Ike" Clanton and his sons, local cattlemen who relied mainly upon stealing cattle from Mexico and holding up stagecoaches and railroads to make a profit, a powerful group of killers and gunmen assembled in the area. Notorious outlaws like Curly Bill Brocius and Johnny Ringo eagerly awaited a chance to square off with the famous Wyatt Earp. Like the Earp group, the ranchers also lived under the protection of the law by enlisting the support of Tombstone resident John Behan, sheriff of Cochise County.

A bitter personal feud quickly developed between Wyatt and Behan. The two ran against each other in an 1881 election for the office of county sheriff that witnessed heated accusations flying from one camp to the other. Republican Earp charged that Behan protected the Clantons from arrest, while Democratic Behan countered that the Earp brothers and Doc Holliday were involved in illegal acts.

The antagonism intensifed after the election, which Behan won. Wyatt struck up a close relationship with Josephine Marcus, a stunning beauty who dumped her previous companion—John Behan—for Wyatt. Josephine later explained that "Wyatt was a man, a fact that made me see that Johnny had been something less. I soon forgot all about Johnny." The two men worked for the same law, but kept a wary eye out for the other.

This photograph of Wyatt, taken in Tombstone, shows the proud, determined side of the lawman.

Events now propelled the Earps and the Clantons along the path that ended in bloodshed. Wyatt found one of his missing horses in Billy Clanton's possession and forced him to hand it back. Virgil and Wyatt led a posse in search of six mules, stolen from a nearby Army post, and located them at the farm of the McLaurys, friends of the Clantons. The McLaurys agreed to pay a stiff fine to avoid going to jail.

A string of stagecoach robberies occurring in the first half of 1881 stirred further controversy. The Earps claimed Ike Clanton planned every job, and charged that the Clantons avoided jail only because of their connections with Sheriff Behan. Behan hotly denied the accusations and answered that the Earps, and especially Doc Holliday, had set up each robbery, including one where the bandits killed the stagecoach driver and one of the passengers. Behan even arrested Holliday over it.

Though Judge Wells Spicer quickly freed Earp's friend, animosity between the groups intensified to such a dangerous level that Behan swore in a large group of gunmen as undersheriffs. Wyatt, who received support from the Tombstone Law and Order League and the Tombstone *Epitaph*, knew he could count on his brothers, Virgil and Morgan, and the ever-loyal Doc Holliday.

Virgil inflamed the growing crisis by arresting two of Behan's deputies, gunmen Pete Spence and Frank Stilwell, as accomplices in the stagecoach robberies. In September, Frank McLaury met Morgan on the streets. After unsuccessfully challenging the Earp brother to a gunfight, McLaury warned, "If you ever come after me, you'll never take me."

Nerves, already frayed by a stream of hostile encounters, were ready to snap. When they did, the violence unleashed would be frightening.

On October 25, Doc Holliday and Ike Clanton engaged in their own shouting match. Doc screamed at Ike that he was sick of the Clantons spreading lies about the Earps and him and told Ike to use his pistol. When Ike replied that he was unarmed, Holliday called him a liar and claimed that he was too cowardly to fight. Wyatt and his brothers rushed up and separated the two, but the incident triggered emotions that spilled over to the next day.

Ike Clanton headed for one of Tombstone's saloons, where far into the night he drank and muttered insults about the Earps and Doc Holliday. He boasted that he and his friends would finish the matter in a showdown the next day—October 26.

John Behan, the sheriff of Cochise County, battled Earp for control in Tombstone.

THIRTY SECONDS
OF VIOLENCE

Wednesday, October 26 began with threats and ended with bloodshed. About 11:30 a.m. Ned Boyle, a bartender at Wyatt's saloon, the Oriental, woke up his boss to tell him that Ike Clanton had been bragging that "as soon as the Earps make their appearance on the street today, the ball will open." Wyatt hurried out to find Virgil, then started to hunt for Ike.

Virgil spotted Ike Clanton in an alley and, after carefully stepping up from behind, grabbed Ike's rifle from his grasp. Ike went for his six-shooter, but Virgil knocked him to his knees with a quick blow to the head.

"You been hunting for me?" Virgil snarled at the dazed cowboy.

The famous O.K. Corral. Many people still erroneously believe the violent gun battle occurred at this spot.

Joseph Isaac "Ike" Clanton, a local cattle rustler, detested Wyatt and his brothers.

"If I'd seen you a second sooner I'd of killed you," Ike mumbled.

Virgil arrested Clanton for possession of firearms and hauled him off to the courthouse.

Word quickly spread throughout the town that the building tension between the Earps and Clantons seemed headed for an explosion. Wyatt met Ike Clanton sitting outside the courtroom and warned, "You've threatened my life two or three times. I want this thing stopped."

When Ike refused to back down, Wyatt heatedly added, "You dirty cow thief, if you're anxious to fight, I'll meet you."

"I'll see you after I get through here," Ike shot back. "All I want is four feet of ground."

As Wyatt walked outside the courthouse, an angry Tom McLaury challenged him to a fight. Wyatt wasted little time on his assailant, though. Yelling angrily, "All right, make a fight right here!" Wyatt pulled out his gun, slapped McLaury's face with his left hand, and cracked McLaury across the temple with the gun. A nearly unconscious McLaury slumped to the ground. Wyatt left McLaury where he lay and walked on to find brothers Morgan and Virgil.

About 2:00 p.m. Behan was getting a shave from a barber when he noticed a crowd gathering outside. When Behan spotted the three Earp brothers just beyond the onlookers, he realized violence could break out at any moment and rushed outside to prevent any bloodshed. After telling Virgil he would disarm the Clantons and pleading for a few minutes to do so, Behan hastened away. The Earps waited a short time, then started walking to meet their foes.

Before they had advanced very far, Doc Holliday joined the brothers. Wyatt looked at his friend and mentioned, "Doc, this is our fight. There's no call for you to mix in."

Wyatt knew Doc would never abandon him when the chips were down, though. Virgil deputized Holliday and handed him a shotgun.

Slowly, carefully, the group of four armed men walked along the sidewalk up Fourth Street toward Fremont. Dressed totally in black outfits, with black stetson hats and bow ties to match their swooping black mustaches, the four presented an awesome spectacle. Etched across their rugged faces were the determination to end the quarrel and the willingness to use force if necessary.

Tom McLaury could not escape the Earp brothers' wrath.

Upon reaching Fremont Street, they spotted the Clantons talking to Behan near Camillus Fly's Photo Gallery. Leaving the sidewalk, they strode directly up the middle of Fremont Street with slightly hastening footsteps.

Behan was trying to convince the Clantons to back down before the Earps appeared. Ike Clanton and Tom McLaury showed Behan they were not armed, but Billy Clanton and Frank McLaury wore six-shooters and had easy access to a rifle hanging in a scabbard from Frank's horse.

Frank McLaury met a violent end in the gunfight.

Behan begged the men to be sensible. "Boys, you must give me your arms." Frank McLaury said he wanted to avoid a shootout, but he would not allow Behan to disarm him "unless you disarm the Earps." When Wyatt and his group suddenly turned the corner onto Fremont, Behan ordered the Clantons to "stay here," then hurried toward the approaching Earps.

"For God's sake, don't go down there," Behan pled with Virgil, but the situation was far beyond the sheriff's control. Virgil replied, "I'm going to disarm them" and walked with the other three men directly by Behan.

The Clanton group watched Behan's futile effort and started backing into a twenty-foot piece of land between William Harwood's house and Fly's gallery. They stood and waited here, instead of near the O.K. Corral, which was over one hundred feet away.

As the Earp party stepped within six feet of their foes, Billy Claiborne suddenly bolted from his comrades and sought safety inside Fly's shop, leaving four men to face the lawmen. Tom and Frank McLaury stood with their backs to Harwood's house, while Ike and Billy Clanton waited on their left, virtually trapped inside the narrow strip of land.

The next thirty seconds turned into a swirling mass of confusion, shouts, and gunshots. No one knew who said what or which side fired first—all that was for certain was that within one half-minute, three men lay dead on Tombstone's street and another three were wounded.

According to Behan, Wyatt opened the affair
by taunting the Clantons. "You have been looking for a fight, and now you can have it." Wyatt
stated that when they heard the sound of cock-
ing guns and noticed the rifle hanging on Frank's
horse, Virgil shouted, "Hold! I don't mean that.

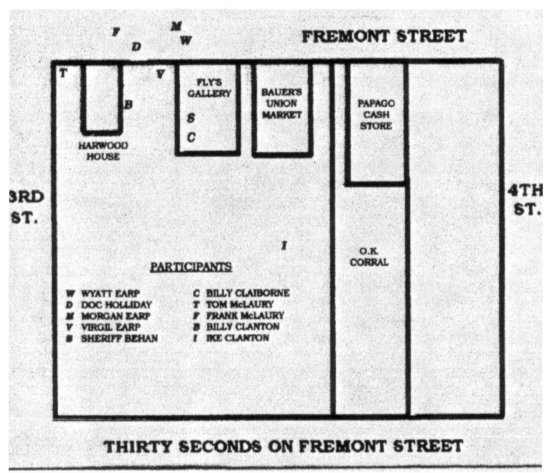

THIRTY SECONDS ON FREMONT STREET

I have come to disarm you," but Billy Clanton
and Frank McLaury supposedly went for their
six-shooters anyway.

"I don't know which shot was fired first,"
Wyatt explained after the fight. "We fired almost
together. The fight then became general."

*As the map shows, the gun-
fight occurred between Fly's
Photo Gallery and the Harwood House, not near the
O.K. Corral.*

While Billy Clanton aimed at Wyatt, Wyatt fired at Frank McLaury, the best gunman opposing him. Billy missed his target, but Earp's shot ripped into Frank's stomach and sent him staggering toward the street. Tom McLaury threw open his vest to show he was unarmed, then hid behind Frank's horse.

A few feet from Wyatt, Morgan took dead aim at Billy Clanton and shot him with such force through the right wrist and in the chest that Billy was slammed against the Harwood house. He slumped to the ground, but continued firing by switching the gun to his left hand and resting the barrel against his arm.

While this unfolded, the unarmed Ike Clanton ran toward Wyatt and grabbed his arm, as if to say he wanted no part of the incident. "Go to fighting or get away," barked Earp. The frightened Clanton sprinted toward Fly's gallery, barely eluding a shotgun blast from Doc Holliday. Clanton dashed through Fly's to the back, and kept running until he found refuge at a dance hall on Allen Street.

The deafening noise scared more than just Ike Clanton. Frank McLaury's horse bolted away, giving Holliday a clear shot at Tom McLaury. Holliday's bullet ripped into McLaury's side with such force that it lifted him into the air. Just as Doc fired, though, he spun around in pain from a bullet that smacked into his hip. Nearby, Morgan Earp shattered Frank McLaury's face with a shot below the ear. McLaury stumbled toward Third Street and died within moments.

The injured Billy Clanton continued firing from the ground near Harwood's house. One shot hit Virgil in the calf, and a second staggered Morgan with a shoulder wound. As Billy attempted to get up, shots from both Wyatt and Morgan sent him sprawling to the ground.

With startling suddenness, the gunshots stopped and a powerful silence enveloped the survivors. As white-grey smoke from the guns drifted toward the sky, Wyatt quickly scanned the scene to determine if any opponent was still capable of fighting. Camillus Fly ran out to the dying Billy Clanton, who begged Fly to give him some more shells, but Fly simply removed the pistol from Billy's hand moments before he died.

In thirty seconds, participants fired an estimated seventeen shots. Three men were wounded—Morgan in the shoulder, Virgil in the leg, and Holliday in the left hip—while Billy Clanton and the McLaurys lay dead on Fremont Street. Only Ike Clanton, who ran away, and Wyatt emerged without a scratch.

Sheriff Behan threatened to arrest Earp's group, but Wyatt simply ignored him and walked by as a crowd of townspeople gathered at the scene. The violence near Harwood's house that would mistakenly go down in history as the Gunfight at the O. K. Corral was over, but the bloodshed had by no means ended.

Billy Clanton wounded Virgil and Morgan Earp before bullets from both Morgan's and Wyatt's guns killed him.

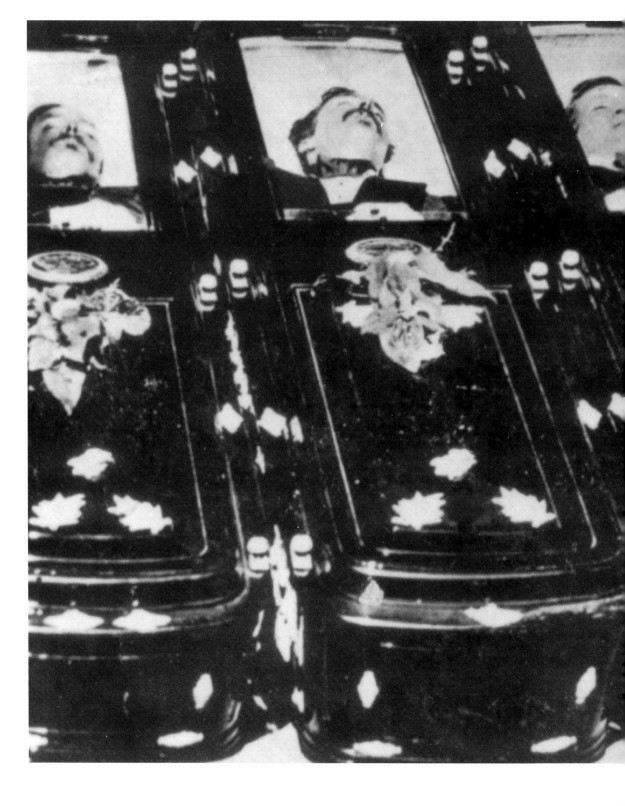

"AS CERTAIN AS DEATH"

Reaction throughout Tombstone and the territory was mixed, depending upon whether one supported the Earps or the Clantons. The *Epitaph* ran a headline proclaiming, "THREE MEN HURLED INTO ETERNITY IN THE DURATION OF A MOMENT." Friends of the Clantons organized an elaborate funeral that included a huge procession through the town. One mourner held a sign stating, "MURDERED IN THE STREETS OF TOMBSTONE." As a precaution, supporters guarded the Earp homes in case someone tried to seek revenge.

Sheriff Behan and Ike Clanton accused Wyatt Earp and Doc Holliday of murder and swore out warrants for their arrest. After listening to thirty days of bitter testimony, Judge Wells Spicer

From left to right, the bodies of Tom McLaury, Frank McLaury, and Billy Clanton lie neatly in a row for mourners to view.

concluded that there was insufficient grounds for charging either man. He criticized Virgil for deputizing Doc Holliday, but concluded the Earps were "officers charged with the duty of arresting and disarming brave and determined men who were experts in the use of firearms, as quick as thought and as certain as death, and who had previously declared their intentions not to be arrested nor disarmed."

One by one Spicer dismissed different accusations. He concluded the Earps had not intended to goad Ike Clanton into a fight so they could kill him, as some contended, since none of the Earp party shot at Ike once the bloodshed started. Spicer added that the criminal reputations of the Clanton gang members and the numerous threats they directed at the Earps cast doubt on any charge they now raised against Wyatt and Doc.

Spicer ended by asserting that the Earps lived in a frontier environment filled with "lawlessness and disregard for human life,...and considering the many threats that have been made against the Earps, I can attach no criminality" to what they had done.

Others did, though, and those hard feelings led to a string of violence that left more dead than the gunfight itself. As Virgil Earp crossed Fifth Street one night in December, hidden assailants ambushed him. Though he lived, his left arm was so mangled from the gunshots that he could no longer use it. When Virgil's wife, Allie, rushed to his side, he comforted her by telling her to "Never mind. I've got one arm left to hug you with."

Though Wyatt increased his vigilance, worse followed. On March 18, 1882 Wyatt walked into Campbell and Hatch's Pool Hall, where brother Morgan was involved in a pool match. He had been worried for Morgan's safety and wanted to be near him should trouble flare. Wyatt sat down to watch the game, when shots suddenly exploded through the glass portion of a door, fatally wounding Morgan. Wyatt rushed outside, but was unable to get a good look at the attackers, who already were riding out of town.

Wyatt returned to the pool hall to check on Morgan, but there was little he could do for his barely-breathing brother. Wyatt bent over, tenderly picked up Morgan, carried him to the coroner's office, and gently placed him on a sofa. Though a doctor rushed to the scene, Morgan died within a few hours.

Frank Stilwell was gunned down only two days after Morgan Earp's death.

Wyatt never doubted who the murderers were and swore vengeance on the Clanton survivors. Gathering his own posse, including brothers Virgil and Warren, Doc Holliday, and two notorious gunmen named Turkey Creek Johnson and Sherman McMasters, Wyatt headed to Tucson to transport Morgan's body to California.

While there, Wyatt learned that one of his brother's supposed killers, Frank Stilwell, was in town. He wasted little time tracking him down and getting revenge for Morgan. On March 20, only two days after Morgan's death, Stilwell was murdered. He was shot at such close range that powder burns covered the six places that bullets entered his body. Though no one witnessed the killing, most people in town held Wyatt and his group responsible.

Wyatt felt no remorse over the deed. He later told his attorney, William Herring, that "I let him have both barrels. They almost tore him apart. I have no regrets; I know I got the man who killed Morg."

Another man said to have been involved in Morgan's murder, Florentino Cruz, was next. Wyatt and his posse located him alone in a wood camp near Tombstone on March 22 and killed him. Within four days of Morgan's murder, Wyatt had disposed of two of his supposed attackers.

Pete Spence, a third man rumored to have taken part in Morgan's death, was next. Wyatt headed back to Tombstone to gun Spence down, but the frightened Spence avoided retribution by surrendering to Sheriff Behan before Wyatt arrived.

Johnny Ringo, one of the West's fastest draws, died in the Arizona desert.

The killing ended in July when Wyatt led his posse into the Arizona desert searching for Curly Bill Brocius and Johnny Ringo. Ringo, a feared gunfighter, was later found dead from a single gunshot to the head. Resting on a tree next to him were his Winchester rifle and his revolver still in its holster. Wyatt claimed he killed Brocius during a furious shootout with a gang of outlaws. Though never proven, no one in Tombstone ever saw Brocius again.

By now, Earp opponents and other Arizona citizens, concerned over the killings, applied tremendous pressure on officials to end the violence. Law officers in nearby Pinal County even issued warrants for the arrest of Wyatt and Doc

Holliday for the murder of Frank Stilwell, which caused Wyatt's attorney to issue hasty advice.

"I advised Wyatt and Doc to get out of Arizona before Sheriff Bob Paul could serve the warrants he had in his possession. They left the Territory in a matter of hours. Warren went with them."

The trio traveled to Gunnison, Colorado. Though the Arizona governor signed legal papers requesting that Wyatt and Holliday be returned to Arizona, Colorado's governor refused to take such action, claiming, "To return these men to Arizona would be equivalent to condemning them to death."

This action, in effect, halted the blood feud between Wyatt Earp and the Clanton faction. Restless as always, Wyatt moved to other locales and opportunities.

AFTERMATH

Wyatt continued his hectic pace for the rest of his life, although he largely remained out of the national spotlight. Though he led a fascinating existence, his role in the Tombstone battles overshadowed anything he would do from then on.

For the next twenty years he and Josephine Marcus journeyed far and wide seeking adventure and wealth. Prospecting ventures in Colorado, Idaho, and Nevada, business deals in Texas and California, and even a three-year stint in Alaska operating a saloon during Nome's gold rush days, handed the couple all the excitement they could want.

They eventually settled into a comfortable retirement in California around 1905, where Wyatt looked after real estate transactions and

Wyatt Earp in the 1920s, when he and Josephine lived in California.

a stable of thoroughbred horses. Living near the fledgling movie industry, Wyatt associated with Hollywood directors and actors, including famed actor William S. Hart, and unsuccessfully attempted to convince them to film his life story.

Wyatt Earp died on January 13, 1929, two months before his eighty-first birthday. After living a life filled with violence, gunfights, and death, Wyatt peacefully passed away in his California home with his beloved Josephine at his side. Ironically, for a man who lived in the midst of violence for much of his life, not one bullet scar marred his towering frame. The lawman's remains were cremated and placed in an Oakland, California cemetery. Fifteen years later, Josephine died and was buried next to Wyatt.

Legend tells us that Wyatt Earp was a famous lawman who helped tame the Wild West. Some biographies, with shameless disregard for fact, build his reputation to monumental size and write of him in almost reverent tones.

If these contain only a semblance of truth, what can one conclude about the man? Like most men and women who braved the hazards of the American West during the latter half of the nineteenth century, Earp was a mixture of good and bad, a man who preferred living within the law but who would not hesitate to take matters into his own hands when necessary. He headed west seeking fortune, whether in prospecting or marshaling; he associated with known killers and con artists; he brutally shot down those responsible for his brother's death. Yet he also brought law and order to unruly cow towns; he gave total loyalty to family and to the few close friends he made; he remained madly in love with Josephine until his final day.

Wyatt and Josephine in more relaxing times in their final years.

Wyatt Earp was a man of his times who, to survive in a difficult era, mixed an unusual combination of ruthlessness with civility. The dual strain produced one of the most fascinating stories to emerge from the West.

CHRONOLOGY

March 19, 1848	Wyatt Earp is born in Monmouth, Illinois
1864	The Earps move to California
January, 1870	Wyatt marries Willa Sutherland
May, 1870	Willa dies of typhus
1871-1873	Wyatt hunts buffalo in Indian Territory
Summer, 1873	Wyatt arrives in Ellsworth, Kansas
April, 1875	Wyatt becomes deputy marshal in Wichita
April 19, 1876	The Wichita city commission fails to rehire Earp
May, 1876	Wyatt is a law officer in Dodge City
Winter, 1876	Wyatt works in Deadwood
July, 1877	Wyatt returns to Dodge City
December, 1879	Wyatt arrives in Tombstone
October 26, 1881	Gunfight at the O.K. Corral
December, 1881	Virgil Earp is wounded
March 18, 1882	Morgan Earp is murdered
March 20, 1882	Frank Stilwell is killed
March 22, 1882	Florentino Cruz is killed
July, 1882	Johnny Ringo and Curly Bill Brocius are killed
July, 1882	Wyatt leaves Tombstone
1905	Wyatt and Josephine settle in California
January 13, 1929	Wyatt Earp dies at age 80
1944	Josephine Marcus Earp dies

FURTHER READING

Boyer, Glenn G. *I Married Wyatt Earp: The Recollections of Josephine Sarah Marcus Earp.* New York: Longmeadow Press, 1994.

DeArment, Robert K. *Bat Masterson: The Man and the Legend.* Norman: University of Oklahoma Press, 1979.

Faragher, John Mack. *"The Tale of Wyatt Earp,"* in Mark C. Carnes, General Editor, *Past Imperfect: History According to the Movies.* New York: Henry Holt and Company, 1995.

Green, Carl R. and William R. Sanford. *Wyatt Earp.* Hillside, New Jersey: Enslow Publishers, Inc., 1992.

Holbrook, Stewart H. *Wyatt Earp, U.S. Marshal.* New York: Random House, 1956.

O'Neal, Bill. *Encyclopedia of Western Gunfighters.* Norman: University of Oklahoma Press, 1979.

Rosa, Joseph G. *Age of the Gunfighter.* New York: Smithmark Publishers, Inc., 1993.

Trachtman, Paul. *The Gunfighters.* New York: Time-Life Books, 1974.

Waters, Frank. *The Earp Brothers of Tombstone.* Lincoln, Nebraska: University of Nebraska Press, 1960.

PICTURE CREDITS

page 2	Arizona Historical Society
6	Corbis-Bettmann
9	Arizona Historical Society
10	Arizona Historical Society
13	Corbis-Bettmann
14	Arizona Historical Society
18	Corbis-Bettmann
20	Corbis-Bettmann
22	Kansas State Historical Society
24	Kansas State Historical Society
27	Kansas State
30	Boot Hill Museum
34	Corbis-Bettmann
36	Arizona Historical Foundation
38	Arizona Historical Society
39	Arizona Historical Society
42	Arizona Historical Society
43	Arizona Historical Society
44	Arizona Historical Society
46	Arizona Historical Society
47	Arizona Historical Society
48	Arizona Historical Society
51	Arizona Historical Society
52	Arizona Historical Society
55	Arizona Historical Society
56	Arizona Historical Society
58	Arizona Historical Society
61	Arizona Historical Society

INDEX

ABOUT THE AUTHOR

John F. Wukovits is a teacher and writer from Trenton, Michigan, who specializes in history and sports. His work has appeared in more than 25 national publications, including *Wild West* and *America's Civil War*. His books include a biography of the World War II commander Admiral Clifton Sprague, and he has written biographies of Barry Sanders, Jesse James, and Vince Lombardi for Chelsea House. A graduate of the University of Notre Dame, Wukovits is the father of three daughters—Amy, Julie, and Karen.